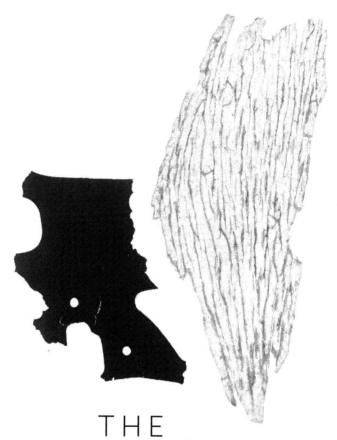

THE GREEN CONDITION

Copyright © 2013 by Elizabeth J. Colen
All rights reserved

Published by Ricochet Editions
www.ricocheteditions.com

Ricochet is an imprint of Gold Line Press, founded in 2012. Our mission is to publish innovative, non-traditional, trans-genre, or genre-less works that have a hard time finding homes in journals, competitions, and with other chapbook publishers. Ricochet is associated with the University of Southern California's Ph.D. program in Creative Writing and Literature.

Ricochet chapbooks are distributed by Small Press Distribution
www.spdbooks.org / 800-869-7553

This title is also available for purchase directly from the publisher

Photography and book design by Robey Clark
Ricochet Editions logo by Dylan Sung

Library of Congress Cataloging-in-Publication Data
Colen, Elizabeth
The Green Condition / Elizabeth Colen

Library of Congress Control Number: 2013947657

ISBN 13: 978-1-938900-07-5

9 8 7 6 5 4 3 2 1

First Edition

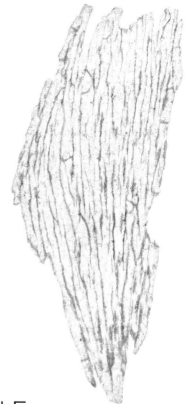

THE GREEN CONDITION

Elizabeth J. Colen

Yesterday I saw a woodpecker whittling a wood door.

Sometimes I knock to come in.

Today I saw two twigs of purple lilac with my house key, three would make it odd. I stand in my backyard and listen for the trees, listen for the raccoon standing in the trees waiting for me to leave.

There are seven requirements for a casting core. The Capitoline Wolf is made of bronze, stands in the Palazzo dei Conservatori on the Campidoglio.

Whether you believe the story behind the statue is beside the point.

The Concise Oxford Dictionary of Current English says raccoon can be spelled racoon, but autocorrect will right it. Dexterous and intelligent, this animal never tires and will eat almost anything: garbage, leaves, insects, bird eggs, other vertebrates.

Other *vertebrates*.
This place is not ideal.

We fight for four days the week we move in. Until no one says anything. There are boxes I never unpack. I have no idea what's in them.

The paint stays half-finished until June.

In the green condition there must be adequate strength for handling.

We move in winter, move *for* winter. Two bedrooms, two
baths, unfinished basement, a lawn. She has a job up north.
Down here is where she wants to be, even though the drive
is long.

The highway, three miles from here, takes at least 17 minutes
to get to.

The dog takes the prime real estate of our back yard. Chews
grass, digs holes in the center of each bed, buries bones and
biscuits, my watch, and one lone shoe: some blue clog left by
a previous tenant.

Animalia, Chordata, Mammalia—
There is evidence of scratching on the lid of every can.
—Carnivora, Procyonidae, Procyon, lotor.

We redefine the morning. She goes into her room, I go in mine. At eight she hits the road.

Week one there are eagles here, a nest on one of the playing field lights. Each day around noon I walk there to try to spot them.

On the third day I think I see the back of a white bird head.

When she leaves I put her toothbrush in my mouth. I hold it there two hours.

There are many ways to build a core—wood, sand, plaster, anything dissolvable.

The dog is often upset at her leaving. If she is in the backyard when the car starts, she whines, knowing. When she comes in she searches every room. To baby this anxiety, or to show love, to calm, I sit outside with her at first, as though we are both getting used to the air outside, the neighborhood without her. Out there we cannot smell her soap, her shampoo, perfume. Out there there are no stray blonde strands populating the sink basin, no blue globs of toothpaste, no tweezer's errant hairs.

Outside we watch for floatplanes. We are in North Seattle, on the westernmost part of the strip of land between Lakes Washington and Union and the slip of Sound that runs between the mainland and Bainbridge Island.

At some angles, a map of Seattle can look striped from north to south. Land, water, land, water, land, water, and then the Olympic Peninsula and then the sea.

I take the garbage out and one of the two handles that secure the lid has been pulled down, the lid is askew, and small bits of plastic bag litter the ground.

The eagle was a symbol of the Roman empire under Augustus, who saw himself as a modern-day Romulus.

And the beep sound of the car horn that secures the car and indicates she's home can get the dog to the door faster than anything, jumping, wagging. And then the patient, expectant sitting, staring at the door.

A lot of cars have this feature.

No matter how many false alarms, the dog gets excited every time.

Rome was built on seven hills: Aventine, Caelian, Capitoline, Esquiline, Palatine, Quirinal, and Viminal.

Seattle was also built on seven hills: First, Second, Yesler, Denny (flattened and sluiced into Elliott Bay, it's now the Denny Regrade), Queen Anne, Beacon, and Capitol.

Crown Hill, which rises behind my neighborhood is an alternate, one of three. Not what the city was built on, but where it expanded.

Floatplanes leave the islands for Lake Union, the closest to downtown, at regular intervals all day. I once counted 47 planes in a six-hour span.

Crown Hill was annexed in 1954; my mother was born in 1953.

Deep in the ground, among seashells, a white eagle mosaic. In Augustus's *Domus Livia*, what was once the Lupercal cave.

We listen for the titter of wrens and house sparrows and white crowned sparrows. The white crowns have more of a song. A regular cadence you can tune in to. When the dog hears it she stops and stares, lifts her chin a little, cocks her head.

The story goes: Romulus and Remus were born to a virgin and, accordingly, were placed in the river to drown. Their mother spent the rest of her short life in chains.

Eaglets are born to the playing field eagles. I hear them up there every day for a week, their small tinny cries.

One day one falls, and then another, so the newspaper says. I imagine finding one there on the field, picking it up, its translucent skin fuzzed white, its tiny black beak, the twitch of its heart slowing steadily in my palm.

Native range in red, introduced are colored blue.

We listen for birdsound. We hear trains. On another house two doors up pigeons gather. The roof is speckled white.

The houses are all so close here and usually the shades are drawn.

I listen hard, but can only hear the pigeon coos if everything else is quiet.

Grandchildren of Numitor, sons of the god of war.

As with everywhere, there are also crows. Who make a racket. Who drop sandwich wrappers and oyster shells on top of my car.

There is also the higher-pitched tittering sound I hadn't recognized at first is not a bird at all.

Fur birds, maybe, my neighbor, Caroline says.

What is that? I ask.

When they're agitated they sound like that, the raccoons.

She tells me one has been living on the back of our block for over a year. She doesn't know where the nest is. I speculate about the tall tree between our yards.

Our back yards border. She runs a daycare. The children are taught to "make big" if they see it, and come right back inside.

I'm too tired to make dinner, but get take-out. I get too much, and eat it alone standing in the kitchen watching the wind blow the trees around and the neighbor's lights go on and off while people move through rooms.

At one point we had a symbiosis. An understanding of how a life should look.

Once I know what to listen for, I hear it all the time.

History is full of abandoned babies. And murder. How Rome got its start.

I am most interested in the bronze sculpture of the wolf, and the core that was made to hold it. The core that was designed to come apart in the end once the casting metal had cooled, held shape.

We met first as friends. The first kiss a few weeks later was to quiet her.

We were in her cabin, sitting on the tile floor with our backs against the bed, talking about all the bad things we had done.

I had been staring at her mouth for at least an hour, watching the words come out and thinking I could love her.

At some point the eagles move on.

I associated with the story immediately: suckled by a she-wolf, destined for history.

A woman stands in her yard across the alley, spinning slowly with a blue and yellow bundle held tightly in her arms.

—

The rains come hard the first few weeks. The rivers swell. And the storm drains all clog with leaves.

—

The river was flooded, high. And when it receded, the babies ended up on the shallow bank.

Carved walnut wood cradle under a fig tree. Found by a she-wolf and a woodpecker, gender unspecified.

—

At first she comes and goes. Leaves most things. Then she starts taking her toothbrush. I don't know where she stays. With a common friend, she says. But I catch her in lies I never mention.

On a good day the drive north to her work is one hour, twenty minutes door to door. On a bad day it can be three hours.

Her legs have developed a soreness.

For health, what can I say? *If you have to stay away, you have to stay away.*

Every night she texts the same message goodnight.

I didn't want to move here.

It is said in conservation, these are creatures of Least Concern.

We don't know where the heart is.

We don't know what to save.

I didn't want to move here, but I'm growing to like it: the water, the planes, the neighbors even. The unexpected quiet.

I find the bakery first. It has ginger biscuits and excellent coffee. From each day's selection of baked goods I imagine what I might bring home to her.

On weekends it is filled with young families and there is a line out the door. On weekdays it's just me and a few old Swedish men who play cards and eat pastries. By my third visit, the men nod as I come in.

On the playing cards: a nautical scene. An anchor with rope and a couple of birds.

The wolf-figure is either fifth century BC Etruscan or thirteenth century AD. The jaunty suckling boys were added in the fifteenth century by artist Antonio del Pollaiolo. He was mostly a painter.

I walk the dog to the park at the end of the marina. It is late afternoon and the rain is constant and we can hear the sea lions barking from the buoys just off the breakwater. The dog gets excited and pulls on her lead.

We walk on the beach and the dunes and the trail through the marshland. We take the trail up to the field.

The lower park and upper park are bisected by train tracks that are only marked in certain spots. I have heard of people getting struck by trains while hiking. These aren't news accounts, but stories people have told me. I listen for trains and keep the dog tethered.

It is said the lower park and the Shilshole Bay Marina will be underwater due to sea rise by the year 2050.

The cavern under the Domus Livia is 15 meters deep and covered with mosaics, pumice stone, and seashells. A probe took the photos. The cave entrance has yet to be found.

I start eating apples because she does. It's her favorite food.

I keep four each of Pink Lady, Gala, Honey Crisp, and Fuji. So she will have them when she's here.

Then I have to eat them so they won't go bad.

West Seattle will be under water too, the beaches and houses. Anything less than eight feet above sea level.

It's where she lived when we first started dating, in a tiny pink house too close to the road. She took my hand and we walked to the water every day.

And one night, reclined on a sun-bleached log of driftwood under the blue light of a nearly full moon, her shirt lifted up and I could see the concentrated constellation of pigmented spots on her abdomen. *Stars*, I said.

And I knew I was changed.

Sometimes I think I hear things under the porch, a scratching sound, some mumbling. When I turn on the light whatever it is disappears.

Many experts deny the recent rediscovery of the cave on topographic and stylistic grounds.

We find out the heart only by dismantling what the heart knows.

My neighbor Lorraine lives up two blocks and has a yard sale almost daily when the rain holds. She's been in her house since 1932. The second week here I buy a pie plate and a tuxedoed doll with impeccable gold hair.

When the sun is out, I stand in the yard. The dog sniffs at a pile of droppings.

Rome's population grew from convicts and runaways, people who couldn't be anywhere else.

The car breaks down or does not break down. In any case, I'm late.

I keep having dreams of being trapped in the unfinished building on campus. All the doors are locked and I can't find the bathroom. Warmth trickles down my leg and the hall smells like new carpet.

Home range sizes vary seven acres for females in cities to twenty square miles for males in prairies.

I find a closet and I squat.

Our lot is .2 acres. The bully unearths the biscuit. When confronted, shows teeth below the mask.

I water beds and trees to make some things grow. The neighbor across the alley builds a rocket out of her newborn's fist.

All the doors are locked and the windows never budge.

The neighbor across the alley doesn't like my dog. She barks, as dogs do. But I never leave her in the yard alone longer than a minute when she's like that because I fear the fight for territory.

The brothers on each of their hills.

The third week some condos burn the next street over. The sky glows red and everyone stands on the sidewalk, looking up.

The best bonfires are built with balled-up newspaper and small sticks for kindling, and logs stacked into an inverted V.

I sit alone with mine, drinking whiskey and eating marshmallows straight from the bag.

Ferries are strips of light that move slow on an invisible horizon. The woody smoke blows inland, burns my eyes.

Across the alley, I watch the neighbor learn about surrender.

She puts the small bundle in the center of the mesh table in her yard. It cries. It shakes its small hands free; they tremble in the space just above its chest. *When do we become whole?* I wonder, thinking: *This isn't it.*

She walks a few paces away before turning back. She slips her finger inside the bright pink baby fist, pulls it up. The crying continues.

I make friends, but I find myself placing personals, filling out profiles online. Every picture obscures my face. People are interested anyway.

You have a way with words, one girl says.

I don't write back.

I am a water sign and have nearly drowned three times.

Phone calls are hard, but texts go through. Sometimes blank ones.

She says she loves me.

I send pictures of where I am, of trees in new bloom, my lunch, of statues on campus. In one, George Washington stands with his back to me, watching the sun set over the Olympic range.

I wait for the green spark, but I have never seen it.

It is an ideal emitter.

The first time was at age five, stuck in mud at the bottom of a neighbor's pond.

The second was at age fifteen, caught in a riptide. My grandmother waved from the shore to swim sideways. Once free of the pull, I lay on my back in the water a few minutes to regain the strength lost to panic before swimming slowly back in.

I was made in secret, and curiously worked in the lowest parts of the earth.

Iman's Superstore is down four blocks on the corner. It is small and open until 9pm and always has a line. One night I get vanilla ice cream and root beer. I read the numbers on the side for the man to put it in the register because the bar code won't scan and he can't find his glasses. The TV is up loud with local news on. I have to repeat the numbers several times. The ice cream is freezer-burnt but still makes a decent float.

The next day at noon a dozen cupcakes arrive in a bright pink box. *Sorry I can't be there today. I am so proud of you*, the card reads.

I stand in the kitchen and eat three in a row, slowly, while staring at the calendar and business cards lining the front of the fridge. I lick the confetti icing first, and then the candy rainbow, which is just colored sugar that melts and leaves its red on my tongue.

The ants start a line toward the box and I put it in the fridge.

The third time on a dare I had jumped from a bridge, some tall span. The river stunned with its cold.

One night we "just miss" each other. I am coming home late from class and the drink that I had after that I said was a conference with a student and she says she needs to drive up north and sleep there to get up early in the morning for a meeting. I am driving home, taking 50th at 50 mph, which is too fast, but I'm catching all the green and no one's in my way. It's like this sometimes when I am late: I can will the traffic to disappear. I want/don't want to see her. I want/don't want to catch her before she leaves. I have delayed. I have had a second drink. Not with anyone, just with myself and a book. I am reading Hopkins. I am memorizing lines. I am looking at the bottles behind the bar called Flowers. I am looking at the pretty bartender who keeps smiling. It is near the university and I am not the only drinker with a book. I am looking in the mirror behind the bar and fingering the thin pages and thinking, how have I never read Hopkins before? And then I notice the mirrored ceiling above me and I am thinking about how my double has been up there the whole time: first drink, second drink. And all the pages. Up there all the time. And then I get in the car and I take 50th too fast. And Phinney too fast past all the zoo signs and all the apartment buildings and storefronts. And I can see the Olympics, their hulking in the near-dark. And she texts me to say she is leaving now. Leaving the house I know she means. But I let myself feel it the other way. And there is a pause in my heart and a space opens up. And with the window down that space fills with cold. And I don't text her back that I am only two minutes away and could she wait. She said the light would be on and it was.

When the ants file in, I do my best to sweep the bulk of them outside. I use one piece of paper to corral them onto another. I stand on the back porch and shake them into the grass.

After, I do better cleaning the kitchen and they never return.

That week it rains hard and the basement floods. I put the dog outside and she barks at the trees and the lady starts screaming again. So I let the dog in and we both pad around in the water.

The lights flicker. And I've forgotten how to make my dead legs work.

There is a scratching under the porch. And a can overturns in the alley.

Week four: we fight. She calls an hour after leaving. I think I can hear the ocean, and some planes. I ask her where she is.

A payphone.

    That's what.

What?

    I asked where.

I forgot my cell phone, she tells me.

I see it on the couch beside me.

Suddenly I want to be there with her, standing on the street or beach or boardwalk, watching planes. I want to hear the dial tone.

The tone stops when the first numeral is dialed.

The wolf stands in a tense and watchful pose.

The sign on the chain-link at 24th and Market says Notice of Cleanup Action, even though the hole where the parking garage will go has already been dug and the concrete poured, the rebar is curling out of it, and the 16-storey crane has arrived.

I watch a short video about how raccoons wash their food, about how much they use their hands. One of the animal handlers puts a paw up close to the camera to show the length of the fingers and complexity of the joints.

There is a hard edge to the counter. I do pushups while I watch and come away with a deep red line across both palms.

The word "raccoon" was adopted from the native Powhatan term, *arathkone* or, alternatively, *aroughcun*, or from Algonquin *ahrah-koon-em: one who rubs, scrubs and scratches with its hands.*

In a crib alone as a baby. Father was working and mother went out.

She can't walk anyway.

In the hardened state it must be strong enough to handle the forces of casting.

Except I fell out once. Ten stitches and two damaged legs.

The baby's tiny fist.

A herdsman named Faustulus found them in the wolf's den, in Lupercal cave. He took them home and raised them as shepherds at the foot of Palatine Hill.

I don't know anyone who wants kids who doesn't already have them.

It gets into everything. It tips over the garbage can every couple of days. I say "it," though there could be more than one.

Animal control wants nothing to do with me.

Call if you trap it, the man says.

And then what?

I set humane traps in the alley. The metal spring tests my patience. I pinch my fingers twice before I find the right resistance.

The raccoon never bites, but sometimes the trap is moved a little from where I set it. Sometimes the food is gone.

My mother threw the phone once, but it was just the receiver. She tried to rip the whole thing off the wall. Yellow plastic hung like a jaundiced eyeball, wires of orbital sinew in an upside-down U.

I was born exactly on my due date, at 5:23am, Central Time in Kansas. On time, a quick birth, and the only planned offspring of my mother's four.

The world's smallest baby was born at 21 weeks and 6 days. Her feet were the size and color of red gummi bears.

And when it swung: the bell sound.

A raccoon gestates for 63 days. The average litter size is three to five young. She could have had so many by now.

I am standing at my window watching strangers walk by outside. Some of them, a lot of them, I've seen before.

My mother is dying. And I haven't told anyone.

We haven't spoken in years.

The rain stops and then it starts up again.

Are they strangers now that I know their faces?

At the Locks on a Sunday. I listen for the trilling bell that means the chamber gates are opening. I watch the boats go twenty-plus feet up and down.

Small children roll down the duck-covered hill.

German tourists have the best shoes, are impeccably dressed.

Old Scandinavian men in lusekofte hold arms of old women in brightly colored setesdalsgenser.

I hear a dozen different languages, nothing I understand.

Wherearethepantyliners and a toast tobigbreasts is all the Japanese I know. And then a few words in French that I can never spell.

And when it swung—

ahrah-koon-em

Week five: a pickup truck hits my door as I exit my car, does not slow. I see my life this time.

When I get inside she asks if I got the plate. Confused, I think about flatware. And then think, oh.

No, I say.

You should have.

The days that she's here we make dinner late, go to bed at the same time.

When I think about the history of some places, I see everything existing at once: she is here, not here, here is the herdsman's small hut, the unpopulated fields, the pastoral, and the chariots running wild. Here is the beach and the dunes and all the cars in the parking lot and here is the water covering it all.

The moment the truck hits I am there and not-there. I am narrowly missed; I am in the way. My face is white and it is red.

My door won't close properly now. I hear the wind in it when I drive fast. I tell myself it's cosmetic. Or that the jaws of life can reach me easier now if I get in a serious accident.

Compromising top framing sets a structure up for a stability failure.

A span of the I-5 bridge over the Skagit collapses after a girder is struck by an oversize load. The driver says he was "crowded."

The detour adds up to an hour to the drive and she delays her trip south again.

That night the lady with the baby stands in her backyard and yells. I don't know what she's angry with.

stability failure, through-truss, offgassing, arathkone, ahrah-koon-em.

I turn these words over in my mouth.

A book, a third drink, Nina Simone on the stereo behind the bar. The melted ice makes the whiskey go light in my glass.

We combined our names once and built an orchard: five apple, two pear, five cherry, one fig. I became the patron saint of fruit trees. I let the yard grow wild and the ladybugs thrive.

Sit down. There.

The girl's eyebrows flutter when she's nervous.

The aphids stop curling the young leaves.

To retain the core, the dismantling is structured, the teardown, careful.

You don't waste any time.

I was only supposed to kiss her. But oh how the blood flows, nosing through the hull.

It is not coincidence. Aphids are domesticated by ants.

They move them tree to tree for the sweet they excrete when well fed.

Radio frequency is a rate of oscillation.
For other uses, see oscillator (disambiguation) and oscillation (mathematics).

I walk home after. The streets are dark. No busses run. Smoke stays in my hair. She texts the same message goodnight.

What we said once: we *coalesce*.

Are we not fearfully and wonderfully made.

That week the spring tides: the water recedes far into the bay and the mudflats shine until just before dawn.

Top chords fold if their joints get misaligned.

It was all about the birds, the solicitation of formal auspices, the ritual space. Every night, the same message.

The truck hit and the bridge fell in. Only two cars in the river and nobody died.

The brothers on each of their hills.

One stood on Aventine Hill, counting birds. One on Palatine. To determine placement of the new home they would build.

I think about the time my mother let me lean full-bodied against the glass on the top floor of a very tall building. I think about the glass's vibration.

All week the neighborhood paper has been talking about the return of the snowy owl. They aren't supposed to be here. Exotic, they say. Displaced. They come from the arctic. Aggressive, they take out crows and seagulls in battles that leave the eviscerated birds to fall from the sky. On top of Crown Hill, in Sunset Park, I scan tall trees and rooftops of million-dollar houses in search of the owl.

My feet were on the rail.

Two cars and no one died.

The air comes stiff off the waves, wind and water disciplinarian and me helpless on the shore, my feet then knees then hips wandering in.

A common dream is drowning. A common dream: teeth falling out. Sometimes I lose mine to the river.

My father, nervous. *What if the glass breaks?*

From one tall pine, the snowy owl watches for lemmings in the hillside scrub. Sea lions moan in the distance.

Then we'll let her fall.

The jagged span of the Olympics begins to disappear in the clouds.

Week six, I see the raccoon for the first time in the evening near-dark. On two legs, it works at something in the neighbor's fence, clawing a hole there perhaps or sharpening claws. The streetlamp has not come on yet and the neighbor's house is dark. The eyes shine two points of light as my car turns. Just for a second I see white fur on the ears, white fur around its nose, its robber baron mask, greyblack body, striped tail. When I get out of my car it is still there. I hear the scratching, irregular, and then a pause when my door shuts.

Though there is no way to actually see this, I feel that it turns towards me silently, witnessing my arrival, my locking the car, my getting the mail.

I go up the steps and disappear into the house. All night I wonder what it does out there. If the fence has succumbed to whatever it was it wanted. If the food is plentiful, fresh, what kind. How high the trees are and what it sees with its silver untame eyes.

She stands on her toes and is taller, looks down on me.

I see her twice in one week before I tell myself *no*.

The raccoon has a body built for climbing and can drop from a height of 40 feet and walk away unscathed.

After I learn this I stop standing under the hemlock.

One night I dream about the raccoon. I replay the scene of first sighting exactly.

Week seven we go to the beach and I lose my shoes. We never go together again.

The same week I accompany a friend to her abortion. I ask how far along she is so I can imagine its size.

Does it matter?

The absolute refractory period is the interval during which a second action potential cannot be initiated, no matter how large the stimulus.

Good refractoriness is required as the core is usually surrounded by hot metal during molding.

Seven or eight weeks. Blueberry or raspberry. The baby was made when I first got here, I think. And then: not a baby.

After, she's tired. I drive her home.

The rain stops and then it starts again. She sleeps the whole way.

In traffic on Aurora, I flit through stations. Every song is terrible or sad. And NPR is talking about language acquisition in children.

I start reading Walter Benjamin. No one told me which book to read, only that his thinking on aesthetics is vital. That he is a "good person to read."

Going by titles, I choose *The Arcades Project*. But I can't get through a whole paragraph without forgetting what is being talked about.

This might not be his fault, but I will blame him.

Every night she texts the same message goodnight.

Two raccoons make a nest at the top of the crane at 24th and Market, 150 feet up in the air. Construction has stopped and wildlife experts have been unable to capture them.

The lenticular clouds over the hills are saucers of light.

Once we stopped for breakfast without planning anything, which is unlike us. We were just walking and then breakfast happened.

She ordered oatmeal; I ordered pancakes. She got bacon; I got the fake kind. The blueberries were bad in that they were not ripe yet. They made the short stack bitter.

After a few weeks: the temporary span is put in place where the bridge used to be.

For the first hour the engineers stand on the shoulder and watch.

I go to the beach alone again. I lose my phone. I convince a handsome stranger to call me until I find myself. When he leaves he asks for my number.

Permeability must be very high. Escape velocity.

Something to leave the house.

The girl has certain charms. A book collection I can stare into when I've got nothing to say.

A mouth I'd like to live in.

One night the raccoon bares its teeth, chases the dog, who makes a noise I've never heard before. I yell. I bring a broom. The animal turns and faces me. I have on socks and no shoes. I kick its hoary side and it returns to tree. The top of my foot retains a physical echo of the creature's hard round side for hours.

The dentition, 40 teeth with the dental formula: 3.1.4.2 / 3.1.4.2, is adapted to an omnivorous diet. The carnassials are not as sharp and pointed as those of a full-time carnivore.

The rest of the night I image-search animal bites and read about rabies. I read about malaise and pain, craze, hydrophobia, and the paralytic post-furious stage.

It can lie dormant for up to five years.

The world's smallest baby was born without ears.

That isn't true.

I don't know anyone who wants children.

The lemmings scatter, startled, on their way to the sea.

The rain stopped and then it started again. And what of

her mouth. I let my hair go slack in the rain. And what of her mouth. She stood on her toes. *No*, I told her, but then proceeded to *yes*.

At the sex club I forget it all while watching a man tied to a post.

I can only see a penis like this, a butch girl tells me.

I smile with a look I hope says *thank you*, this connection. I want to touch the scar on her face. But I'm not going home with her.

Are we not fearfully and wonderfully made.

And later at the fence I pass two cupcakes over, furtively.

I imagine my neighbor standing in the kitchen licking the icing slowly, peeling the paper back.

She stands on her toes and looks down on me.

If watching's what you want, sweetheart, I can make that happen.

I make it a point to say nothing. But I'm there when she calls.

If you won't fuck me... She kisses the girl in front of me, then gets her down on her knees.

But she was hoping I would give in if another girl were involved. And looks at me like, *This could be you.*

She got a pretty one. Both in black lace. Both with black hair. Two beautiful girls. Two beautiful mouths.

Oh how the blood flows.

I make myself small in the chair by the door.

It makes sense I would bleed.

I hammer my thumb, trying to make things nice. I want to be home.

And the thumb swells up red under the nail.

Are we not fearfully and wonderfully made.

I start to say *I feel lost here and I'm going to go home*.

But there is nowhere to go.

Across the alley, my neighbor puts the small bundle in the center of the mesh table in her yard. She walks a few paces away before turning back.

We don't know where the heart is.

My mother wants to know if I can get divorced.

I don't mean if you want to, I mean if you are capable. Like, how that works.

I put the *I* and *you* in there, but I am only imagining the conversation.

The best blackberries I've ever eaten grow under the complex A-frame of an electrical tower. The span of towers cuts a narrow slit of field between two dark sets of woods. Brambles grow between and up the metal legs.

Arm hairs stand vertical when you're there, and you can hear the power humming the whole time.

Every night she texts the same message goodnight.

Week eight the neighbor lady with the baby goes crazy. It is 9pm when she beats on our front door, screaming.

I am alone. Or rather, it is just me and the dog. The dog is riled, but takes my cue and stays silent. We both just stare. Through the tiny windows at the top of the door I see the frizz of the neighbor's blonde hair, usually so kempt.

I am sorry, I whisper. *Sorry sorry sorry.*

As the casting or molding cools the core must be weak enough to break down as the material shrinks. Moreover, it must be easy to remove during shakeout.

The funny thing is, I was lonely. She was outside my door, I was inside my door. Human-to-human, I thought. There is a human only five feet away. I thought about opening the door. I thought about what I would say. Maybe, *I know you're busy with the baby and everything, but I have a selection of teas.*

Everything about my mother happens second-hand through my aunts, her sisters. We haven't spoken in fifteen years. Nobody understands it and everybody gets tired of suggesting we make up because there isn't anything to make up except the time she tried to kill me, which my aunt says never happened.

A smooth surface finish.

Ears bordered in white fur. White back of the head.

And also all the childhood stuff, but we were both kids then.

There is a raccoon dead in the alley, blood around its mouth. Is this what I wished for. I call animal control. They say they will send someone out.

When I peek out the gate an hour later, the animal is gone.

As I stood on the bridge, the traffic ran one way.

The next day another neighbor talks about the stress of newborns. The neighborhood hosts a parade and the children sing *Ja, vi elsker* over and over.

Yes, we love. Yes, we love.

NOTES

"We find out the heart only by dismantling what the heart knows" comes from Jack Gilbert's "Tear It Down."

"Are we not fearfully and wonderfully made" and "I feel lost here and I'm going to go home" come from C.D. Wright's *Deepstep Come Shining*.

"I was made in secret, and curiously worked in the lowest parts of the earth" comes from Psalm 139.

"In the green condition there must be adequate strength for handling," "In the hardened state it must be strong enough to handle the forces of casting," "As the casting or molding cools the core must be weak enough to break down as the material shrinks. Moreover, they must be easy to remove during shakeout," "Good refractoriness is required as the core is usually surrounded by hot metal during molding," and "A smooth surface finish" come from Paul E. Degarmo, JT Black, and Ronald A. Kohser's *Materials and Processes in Manufacturing*.

Elizabeth J. Colen is the author of the poetry collections *Money for Sunsets* (STEEL TOE BOOKS, 2010) and *Waiting Up for the End of the World: Conspiracies* (JADED IBIS PRESS, 2012), as well as flash fiction collection *Dear Mother Monster, Dear Daughter Mistake* (ROSE METAL PRESS, 2011). She lives in Seattle.